Earth

by Cody Crane

Content Consultant
Kevin Manning
Astronomer

Reading Consultant
Jeanne M. Clidas, Ph.D.
Reading Specialist

Children's Press®
An Imprint of Scholastic Inc.

Library of Congress Cataloging-in-Publication Data
Names: Crane, Cody, author.
Title: Earth/by Cody Crane.
Other titles: Rookie read-about science.
Description: New York: Children's Press, an imprint of
Scholastic Inc.,
2018. | Series: Rookie read-about science | Includes index.
Identifiers: LCCN 2017028044| ISBN 9780531230848
(library binding) | ISBN 9780531228616 (pbk.)
Subjects: LCSH: Earth (Planet)—Juvenile literature.
Classification: LCC QB631.4 .C73 2018 | DDC 525—dc23
LC record available at https://lccn.loc.gov/2017028044

Produced by Spooky Cheetah Press
Art direction: Tom Carling, Carling Design Inc.
Creative direction: Judith Christ-Lafond for Scholastic

Published in 2018 by Children's Press, an imprint of
Scholastic Inc.

Printed in Heshan, China 62

1 2 3 4 5 6 7 8 9 10 R 27 26 25 24 23 22 21 20 19 18

Photos ©: cover Earth: Donald E. Carroll/Getty Images;
cover background: Kozachenko Maksym/Shutterstock;
back cover: Dr Morley Read/Shutterstock; cartoon dog
throughout: Kelly Kennedy; 1: NASA/Getty Images; 2:
Philip Lee Harvey/age fotostock; 3: Philip Lee Harvey/age
fotostock; 4-5 background: Ingram Publishing/Thinkstock; 5
Earth: Goddard Space Flight Center/NASA; 7 background:
Clearviewstock/Dreamstime; 7 center: Webspark/
Shutterstock; 8: Juliengrondin/Dreamstime; 9: Iofoto/
Dreamstime; 10-11: John Anderson/Dreamstime; 12: JSC/
NASA; 13: Chad Baker/Thinkstock; 14-15: Magictorch; 16:
Thomas Marent/Minden Pictures; 17: Thomas Marent/
Minden Pictures; 19: PSL Images/Alamy Images; 20:
Tigatelu/iStockphoto; 22: ttsz/iStockphoto; 23: Bill Oxford/
iStockphoto; 24 background: NASA; 24 inset: NASA;
26: B. Tafreshi (twanight.org (http://twanight.org))/ESO
Science Outreach Network; 28 paperclip: Angela Jones/
Dreamstime; 28 graph paper: Natbasil/Dreamstime; 28-29:
Aimee Herring; 30 background: Giraphics/Dreamstime;
30 left: Mondadori Portfolio via Getty Images/Newscom;
30 right: Ernest Smith/The Granger Collection; 31 center
top: moodboard/Thinkstock; 31 center bottom: peepo/
iStockphoto; 31 top: JSC/NASA; 31 bottom: Magictorch;
32: NASA.

Scholastic Inc., 557 Broadway,
New York, NY 10012

Table of Contents

Let's Explore Earth!

Does this planet look familiar? It is Earth. More than 7 billion people live here, and you are one of them. Many plants and animals live on Earth, too. Our planet is special. It has water, air, and sunlight— everything creatures need to live.

clouds

I am Rocket. Let's explore this beautiful planet together. It is Earth, your home.

water

land

1

Earth Inside and Out

Earth is a big ball of rock, about 8,000 miles (13,000 kilometers) wide. Inside, our planet has many layers. Earth's superhot inner core is at its center. It can get hotter than the surface of the sun! Beyond that is the outer core. And then there is the mantle. Earth's crust is a thin outer layer that sits on top of the mantle.

Look Inside Earth

Earth is made up of different layers.

crust
Earth's thin outer layer

mantle
made up of gooey rock

outer core
layer of hot, melted metals

inner core
contains superhot, solid metals; can reach 12,600°F (7,000°C)

Earth's crust is made up of giant slabs of rock called tectonic plates. These plates float on top of melted rock in the mantle. Moving plates can rub against each other. That can trigger earthquakes.

Plates can push together to form mountains. Melted rock can erupt from beneath plates, causing volcanoes.

The Hawaiian islands are actually the tops of underwater volcanoes.

Earth's land is divided into seven **continents**. They are surrounded by water. There is more water on our planet than land. Oceans cover two-thirds of Earth! They are filled with salt water. There are rivers, lakes, and ice, too. They contain freshwater. Water is something all life needs to survive.

Earth is the only planet known to have large amounts of flowing water on its surface.

Coral reefs like this one are filled with sea life.

The atmosphere looks like a blue haze surrounding Earth.

atmosphere

There is no air in space.

An **atmosphere** surrounds our planet. It contains the air we breathe. It protects us by blocking dangerous rays from the sun. Those could be harmful to life. The atmosphere stops space rocks headed for Earth. Most burn up in the atmosphere before they can crash into the planet.

Shooting stars are really space rocks called meteors. They burn up as they pass through Earth's atmosphere.

2

Welcome Home

The sun is the center of our solar system. Earth and seven other planets **orbit** around it. Earth's distance from our sun makes it just right for life. It does not get too hot or too cold.

sun

Venus

Mars

Jupiter

Mercury

Earth

Earth is the fifth-largest planet and the third planet from the sun.

Neptune

Uranus

Saturn

Earth is one of eight planets in our solar system.

Heat from the sun makes life on Earth possible. The same is true for its light. Plants need sunlight to grow. Plants then become food

Millions of types of plants and animals live on Earth. These mountain gorillas are found in Africa.

for animals. Other creatures hunt plant-eating animals. Without sunlight, none of those living things, including us, would exist.

Planet on the Move

It takes Earth 365¼ days to orbit the sun. That is one year. The Earth is also spinning as it moves along that path. It takes Earth 24 hours to make one spin. That is one day. Different parts of the planet face the sun as Earth spins. It becomes day there. It becomes night when those parts of Earth turn away from the sun.

Earth spins at about 1,000 miles (1,600 kilometers) per hour near its middle. I bet you never noticed!

Electric lights from cities can be seen glowing on the nighttime side of Earth.

19

Earth's Seasons

Earth's tilt creates seasons. The seasons are opposite in areas above and below the equator.

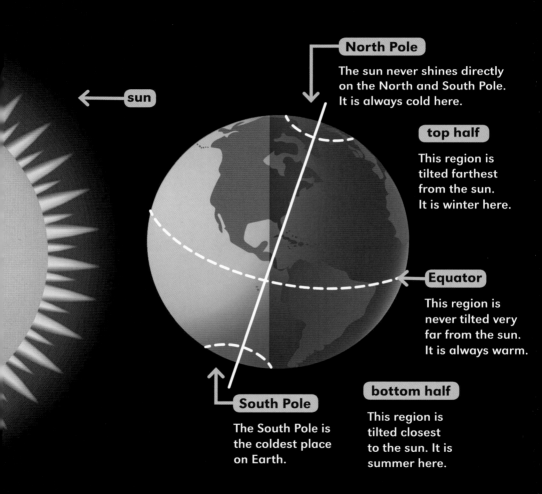

sun

North Pole

The sun never shines directly on the North and South Pole. It is always cold here.

top half

This region is tilted farthest from the sun. It is winter here.

Equator

This region is never tilted very far from the sun. It is always warm.

South Pole

The South Pole is the coldest place on Earth.

bottom half

This region is tilted closest to the sun. It is summer here.

Earth is not perfectly centered in space. It is tilted. So the top and the bottom of Earth lean toward or away from the sun at different times of the year. That is why Earth has seasons. Places near Earth's equator, or middle, are always titled close to the sun. Those places do not have seasons. They stay warm all year!

Other planets in our solar system are tilted. They have seasons as well!

Beyond Earth

The closest object to Earth is the moon. The moon is a smaller rocky ball that orbits our planet. Earth's **gravity** keeps the moon close. The moon's gravity affects Earth, too. It tugs on the planet's oceans. That causes high and low tides.

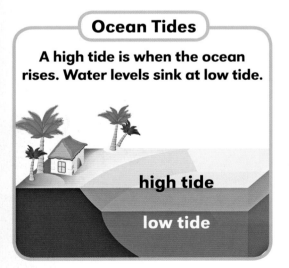

Ocean Tides

A high tide is when the ocean rises. Water levels sink at low tide.

high tide

low tide

It would take six months to get to the moon if you could drive there in a car!

The moon is about one-fourth the size of Earth.

American astronaut Karen Nyberg floats aboard the ISS.

The ISS orbits about 250 miles (400 km) above Earth.

People have visited only one place in our solar system besides Earth. That is the moon. Astronauts first walked on its surface in 1969.

Astronauts also travel to the International Space Station (ISS). The ISS is a science lab that orbits our planet. Astronauts from all over the world live and work there.

The International Space Station has lots of room. It is larger than a six-bedroom house!

Some telescopes use many large dishes to detect signals from space.

Scientists use telescopes to see far into space. They also send spacecraft to study stars and other planets. But they have yet to find anyplace exactly like Earth. Some spacecraft search for other places with life in our solar system—and beyond! Worlds with alien life could be out there, just waiting to be discovered.

What do you think? Is there life on other planets?

Make Tectonic Plates

Discover how Earth's surface moves. Be sure to ask an adult for help!

YOU WILL NEED:
- ✓ 2 feet of waxed paper
- ✓ Plastic knife
- ✓ 8 ounces of frosting
- ✓ 2 graham crackers
- ✓ Eyedropper
- ✓ Water

STEP-BY-STEP:

1 Lay the waxed paper on a flat surface. Spread a thick layer of frosting on top. This is Earth's mantle, made of melted rock.

2 Place the graham crackers next to each other on the frosting. Their edges should touch. These are Earth's tectonic plates.

3

Push the graham crackers away from each other. Watch what happens to the melted rock. Real melted rock would harden into new crust when it cooled.

4

Place the crackers side by side. Slide them past each other. Earthquakes often occur where tectonic plates scrape by each other like this.

5

Reset the graham crackers and push them toward each other. Let one slide underneath the other. When Earth's plates do this, the lower plate melts back into the hot mantle.

6

Use the eyedropper and water to moisten the edge of a cracker. Push the crackers into each other. This is how mountains are formed.

Stories About Earth

People have lived on Earth for millions of years. Over the ages, they came up with stories to explain how our planet came to be.

⭐ The ancient Greeks viewed Earth as a mother. They called her Gaia (GUY-uh). She was thought to have created everything in the world.

Native American tribes told stories of animals that swam to the bottom of the ocean. They brought up mud that became Earth's land.

Glossary

atmosphere (**at**-muhs-feer):
layer of gases that surrounds
a planet

continents
(**kahn**-tuh-nuhnts): seven
large landmasses of Earth

gravity (**grav**-ih-tee):
force that pulls things toward
each other; there is very little
gravity in space

orbit (**or**-bit): travel in a
circular path around a planet
or the sun

Index

Facts for Now

Visit this Scholastic Web site for more information on Earth:
www.factsfornow.scholastic.com
Enter the keyword Earth

About the Author

Cody Crane is an award-winning nonfiction children's writer.
From a young age, she was set on becoming a scientist. She later
discovered that writing about science could be just as fun as the
real thing. She lives in Houston, Texas, with her husband and son.